A Business Trip to New York

I Talk You Talk Press

CONTENTS

INTRODUCTION

The words in **bold** are useful business trip phrases.

You might hear these phrases, and you can use some of these phrases when you go on a business trip.

Carlos is a businessman from Buenos Aires, Argentina. He works for an American drinks company. He is going on a business trip to the company head office in New York. He will stay for four nights.

1. ARRIVAL AND TAXI

Now, Carlos is at the airport in New York. It is late in the afternoon. He is very tired. The flight from Buenos Aires was very long. He had to transfer in Mexico City. He picks up his suitcase and walks out of the airport. He sees a taxi stand. There are some people waiting for taxis. He stands in line and waits. A taxi comes. The driver helps him to put his suitcase in the taxi. He gets in the taxi.

"**Where are you going?**" asks the driver.

"**To** the Central Hotel on Thirty-fourth Street in Manhattan. **How much will it cost?**"

"It will be about fifty-eight dollars," says the driver.

"OK," says Carlos.

The taxi starts to move. He looks out of the window. He is tired, but he is also excited. It is his first time to visit New York.

The buildings are so tall! This is like in the movies! he thinks. There are many people in the streets, and there are many cars.

He arrives at the hotel, and the driver takes the suitcase out of the taxi.

"**Here you are,**" he says to the driver. He gives him the fare and a tip.

"**Thanks,**" says the driver.

Carlos picks his bag up and walks into the hotel.

2. CHECK-IN

Carlos walks into the hotel lobby and goes to the reception desk.

"**Good afternoon,** Sir," says the man at reception.

"**Good afternoon. I have a reservation. My name is** Carlos Castro."

"Yes Sir, **just a moment…**" The man looks at the computer. "Ah, yes, Mr Carlos Castro. You are staying for four nights. Is that right?"

"Yes, that's right."

"OK, Mr Castro. **Could you fill out this form please?**"

"Sure."

Carlos writes his name, address and passport number on the form. He gives it back to the man.

"Thank you, Sir. **Here's your key. Your room number is** three five six. It's on the third floor. The elevators are over there," says the man.

"Thank you," says Carlos. "**What time is breakfast served?**"

"**It's served from** six am **to** ten am in the dining room. The dining room is next to the elevator."

"OK, thanks. **Is there WIFI in the room?**" asks Carlos.

"Yes, of course. Every room has free WIFI."

"OK, thank you."

Carlos picks up his bag and walks to the elevator. He goes to the third floor and finds his hotel room. He goes into his room and switches on the lights.

3. CALLING THE OFFICE

Carlos puts his bag down and takes his smartphone and computer out of his briefcase.

I have to call the New York office, he thinks. He finds the office number on his phone and calls it.

"**Hello, this is** Carlos Castro from the Buenos Aires office. **Could I speak to** the International Manager Mr Khan, **please?**"

"**I'm afraid** Mr Kahn **is in a meeting at the moment,**" says the receptionist.

"**What time will he be free?**" asks Carlos.

"In about an hour. **Can I take a message?**" says the receptionist.

"Yes. **Can you please tell** him **that I called?** I have arrived in New York. **I will call back in** about an hour."

"Yes, of course Mr Castro. **Thank you for calling.**"

"Thank you. Bye."

Carlos switches on his computer. He is tired, but he has to practise his presentation for tomorrow. It is his first time to give a presentation in English. He opens the PowerPoint file and starts to practise his presentation.

He looks at his phone. An hour has passed.

I should call Mr Khan again, he thinks. He calls the office.

"**Hello, this is** Carlos Castro speaking. **Could I speak to** Mr Khan, **please?**"

"**Yes, certainly. Just a moment please.**"

Carlos waits for about 10 seconds. Then, the receptionist says, "I'm sorry, Mr Castro, but Mr Khan **is on another line at the** moment."

What is another line? thinks Carlos.

"I'm sorry, I don't understand. He's on another line?"

"Yes, he's on another telephone. He is talking to another person," says the receptionist.

"Oh, I see."

"I will ask him **to call you back. Can I have your telephone number please?"** asks the receptionist.

"Yes, of course," says Carlos.

Carlos tells the receptionist his telephone number.

"OK, thank you. He **will call you back soon,"** says the receptionist.

"Thank you. Bye," says Carlos.

Carlos lies on the bed, and soon falls asleep.

Carlos wakes up. His phone is ringing. He looks at it.

Oh, it's Mr Khan! he thinks. He answers it.

"Hello, Carlos Castro speaking."

"Hi, Carlos, this is Dave Khan."

"Hello Mr Khan. **Thank you for calling me back. I called before, but you were in a meeting."**

"Yeah, **I got the message. Thanks for calling.** So, **have you arrived in** New York?"

"Yes, I have. **I arrived** a few hours ago," says Carlos.

"How was your trip?" asks Mr Khan.

"It was good, thanks. But it was very long."

"Did you fly direct to New York?" asks Mr Khan.

"No, I didn't. I transferred in Mexico City."

"Oh, that's a long way! You must be very tired!"

"Yes, I am a little sleepy!" says Carlos.

"Well, have a good rest. We will see you tomorrow."

"What time should I come to the office?" asks Carlos.

"Well, **the meeting will start at** nine thirty, so come before then. If you come at nine, I can introduce you to the other people."

"OK, **I'll be there at** nine," says Carlos.

"Do you have the office address?"

"Yes, I do. And I have a map. But **I'll take a taxi,"** says Carlos.

"OK. **If you have any problems, just call the office.** We will help."

"OK, thanks. See you tomorrow."

"Yeah, see you then."

"Bye."

Carlos switches off his phone. He takes a shower. He goes down to the hotel lobby. There is a coffee shop in the lobby. He has a beer and a sandwich. He goes back to his room. He gets ready for bed. He lies down and falls asleep very quickly.

4. ARRIVING AT THE OFFICE

Carlos gets out of the taxi outside the office. He looks up at the building.

Wow! he thinks. *This is a tall building.* He goes into the lobby. There is a reception desk.

"Good morning, **can I help you?**" asks the woman at the reception desk.

"Yes, **I'm here to visit** Dazzle-oh Drinks."

"**Can I have your name?**" asks the receptionist.

"**Yes, it's** Carlos Castro."

"OK, **just a moment please**."

The receptionist calls the Dazzle-oh Drinks office.

"Hello. There is a Mr Carlos Castro to see you," she says. "OK, sure."

She puts the phone down.

"You can go up," she says. "Dazzle-oh Drinks is **on the** fiftieth **floor**."

"Thank you."

Carlos gets into an elevator and presses the button for the 50th floor. He slept very well last night, and he had a good breakfast, so he is feeling fine.

He gets out of the elevator at the 50th floor and walks into the office. There is a reception desk near the door.

"Good morning. **I'm** Carlos Castro **from** the Buenos Aires office. **I'm here for** a meeting."

"Hi. Dave **is waiting for you. Just a moment please. I'll call** him," says the receptionist.

A few seconds later, Mr Kahn comes to the desk.

"Hi Carlos! **Nice to meet you!**"

They shake hands. "**It's nice to meet you too,** Mr Khan."

"Oh, **please call me** Dave. We use first names in this office."

"OK. Thank you Dave."

Dave looks at the clock. "**We have some time before** the meeting starts. Come on, **I'll introduce you to** some other people."

5. INTRODUCTIONS

They walk into the office. There are about twenty desks. There is a man sitting at a large table. Dave takes Carlos to meet him.

"**This is** Reggie. He is the manager of the design team. Reggie, this is Carlos from Buenos Aires."

Reggie stands up. Reggie and Carlos shake hands.

"Hi, nice to meet you Carlos," says Reggie.

"Nice to meet you too."

A woman walks over to them.

"This is Jackie. She's head of marketing. Her office is over there, near the window," says Dave.

Carlos and Jackie shake hands.

"It's nice to meet you," says Jackie. "**If we have time, I'd like to talk to you about** marketing in Argentina."

"OK, sure," says Carlos.

They walk to the other side of the office.

"This is the kitchen," says Dave. "Help yourself to tea and coffee. And the restroom is over there. I'll take you to the meeting room, so you can get set up."

"Set up?" asks Carlos.

"Yeah, set up your presentation. You are the first to present this morning," says Dave.

"Oh really? OK. How many other people will give presentations?" asks Carlos.

"The managers from the Berlin office, the Seoul office, the Tokyo office, and the Mexico City office, so you, and four other people."

They go into the meeting room, and Carlos sets up his computer at the front near the screen and projector.

Carlos has his data on paper. He wants to give everyone a copy.

He goes into the main office and says to Reggie, "**I need to photocopy** these handouts. **Is there a photocopier I can use?**"

"Sure. It's over there, by the window."

"Thanks."

Carlos photocopies the data and makes the handouts. Then he goes back into the meeting room.

A few people are now in the room. Carlos smiles at a man standing near the door.

"Hi. I'm Carlos Castro from Buenos Aires."

"I'm Junya Takeda from the Tokyo office. Nice to meet you."

"Nice to meet you too. **What should I call you?**" asks Carlos.

"**You can call me** Junya. Junya **is my first name.**"

"OK, thanks."

"What should I call you?" asks Junya.

"**Please call me** Carlos. Carlos **is my first name**, and Castro **is my last name.** Dave said the people in this office use first names."

"Yes, they do. **Is this your first time to come here?**" asks Junya.

"Yes, it is. **How about you?**"

"**This is my** second **time**. I came last year," says Junya.

Carlos turns around. Dave and some other managers are walking into the room.

"The meeting is going to start," says Junya. "Good luck with your presentation!"

"Thanks! You too!" says Carlos.

6. PRESENTATIONS

"Good morning, everyone. Welcome to New York!" says Dave. "Today, we will have your presentations, and then, tomorrow morning, we will have a meeting about new products. In the afternoon, you will visit our local factory.

"Well, it is the first time for some people to visit our office here in New York, so let's begin with self-introductions. I'll start. I'm Dave Khan, and I'm the International Manager of Dazzle-oh Drinks. I work here, in the company head office. I've been working for Dazzle-oh Drinks for thirteen years. Before I came to the New York office, I was the manager of the San Francisco office. Before that, I worked in sales in San Francisco."

Dave sits down. Next, the manager from Seoul stands up.

"Good morning, everyone. I'm Jihye Lee. I'm the manager of the Seoul office," she says. "I have been working for Dazzle-oh Drinks for six years. I joined the company after I graduated from university in Seattle. This is my second time to attend this meeting. I'm looking forward to hearing all of your ideas."

Next, Carlos stands up. "Good morning. I'm Carlos. I'm the manager of the Buenos Aires office. I joined Dazzle-oh Drinks three years ago. I started in the sales department in Buenos Aires, and I became manager last year. I'm very happy to be here, and I look forward to seeing everyone's presentations. Thank you."

The other managers introduce themselves, and then Dave says, "OK, let's start. Carlos, you are first. Let's hear your presentation."

Carlos goes to the front of the room and stands next to the screen.

He starts the PowerPoint presentation on his computer.

"**Today, I'm going to introduce** the Buenos Aires office, **and also talk about** the drinks market in Argentina. I have handouts with the data for you."

Carlos puts the handouts in the middle of the table. Everyone takes a copy.

"OK, **first I'd like to give you some background information about** the company in Argentina. There are ten employees working in the Buenos Aires office. The office opened three years ago.

"**This is a picture of** the office. And this is a picture of the employees. **All the products we sell are** made in Argentina. Of course, we make and sell the usual range of Dazzle-oh drinks. But we also make drinks just for the Argentinian market.

"We have five main competitors. Our main competitor is Very Thirsty! It is an old company. Two of the other four competitors are also old companies. Then there are two new competitors. One is a Mexican company, and the other one is American. The American company entered the market a year before us.

"In the first year, our sales were very strong. We introduced a new product called Dazzle-oh Estrella. We designed this for the local market. We had a big marketing campaign. We made a TV commercial with a famous actress.

"The commercial was very successful, and our sales were great. This is the commercial."

Everyone watches the commercial.

"In the first year, we had a market share of fifteen percent. This was higher than we expected. Supermarkets and other stores all over Argentina stocked our products.

"In our second year, the rival American company started to make a drink similar to Dazzle-oh Estrella. They had a famous singer in their TV campaign, and they had a very strong social media campaign.

"They had competitions and other campaigns on Facebook and Twitter. Our market share dropped a little to thirteen point five percent.

"Last year, we started to use social media more. We now have a Facebook page, with seventeen thousand likes, and we have over twenty thousand Twitter followers.

"We also released another new product called Dazzle-oh Astro. It was a hit, especially with teenagers. We had prize campaigns. If people shared our photo on Facebook, they had a chance to win a prize.

"**Please look at** page two of the handout. On page two, there is a graph. This graph shows sales from year one to year three. **As you can see**, the sales dropped in year two, and rose again in year three. In year three we were up to eighteen percent of the market. We hope our sales will continue to rise this year. Our target is twenty percent.

"On page three, there is a chart showing the most popular products. Our Dazzle-oh Astro and Dazzle-oh Estrella are very popular with young people. The actress in our commercials is popular with that age group.

"Next, we want to target the thirty to fifty age group. So now we are planning a new campaign.

"We think we can increase sales. As I said, our target for this year is twenty percent of the market, but it is very competitive. We must bring new products to the market to compete with the other companies.

"**If you have any questions, I'll be happy to answer them. Thank you for listening.**"

"Thanks Carlos," says Dave. "**Does anyone have any questions?**"

The German manager Hans says, "Yes. How much of your market share is from the normal Dazzle-oh drinks range and how much is from your two special products?"

"About half our market share is from the normal range and the other half is from our special range. The sales from the normal range of products are steady. If we want to grow, we have to create more special products and market them very well."

"What is the best way to market the new products?" asks Hans.

"I think social media campaigns are very important," says Carlos.

"What image does our brand have in your country?" asks Junya.

"It has a happy and friendly image. It's cool. People like the design on the bottles. It makes people feel good and happy. Young people think our drinks are fashionable, and also a kind of luxury. It looks and tastes great, but it's not too expensive. That is important for people, I think."

"OK, thank you."

"Thanks Carlos," says Dave. "Next, Ricardo from the Mexico City office, please."

Ricardo starts to set up his presentation. Carlos sits down. He is happy because his presentation was very good. He didn't make any mistakes, and everyone seemed very interested. He listens carefully to the other presentations.

At 12:00pm, Dave says, "OK everyone, **let's stop for** lunch. We will continue the presentations after lunch. **Please be back by** one o'clock."

7. LUNCH

"What are you doing for lunch?" Carlos asks Junya.

"I think I'll go to the Italian restaurant across the road. When I was here last year, everyone went there."

"Oh, I see. **May I go with you?**" asks Carlos.

"I think everyone will go there," says Junya.

Everyone from the meeting walks out of the office. They cross the road and go into the Italian restaurant.

Carlos looks at the menu. He is very hungry. The waiter comes.

"What would you like?" he asks.

"I'd like the vegetable pasta with extra cheese, and garlic bread please," says Carlos.

"Sure," says the waiter. **"Anything to drink?"**

"Yes, a coffee and some sparkling water please."

The waiter takes everyone's orders. Carlos is sitting next to Junya and Jihye.

"How long did it take you to get here?" asks Carlos.

"It took me about sixteen hours," says Jihye. "I had to transfer in Tokyo. How about you, Junya?"

"It took me about sixteen hours too. I had to transfer in Chicago. How about you, Carlos?"

"It took me about nineteen hours," says Carlos. "I transferred in Mexico City."

"It's a long way!" says Junya. **"How long are you staying?"**

"Until Sunday. I want to go sightseeing on Saturday. How about you?" asks Carlos.

15

"I'm staying until Saturday. I fly to Vancouver on Saturday morning," says Junya.

"Vancouver? Why?" asks Carlos.

"I'm going to see the new office in Vancouver. I might transfer there in the future, so I want to see it."

"I see."

"I'm staying until Sunday," says Jihye. "I also hope to go sightseeing on Saturday."

Reggie is sitting at the next table. He hears them talking.

"Do you want to go sightseeing on Saturday? I'm free on Saturday. I can take you!" he says.

"Really? That's very kind of you. Thanks!" says Carlos.

"Thanks!" says Jihye.

They eat lunch.

Then, Reggie looks at his watch. "It's nearly one o' clock. We should go back."

They pay for lunch and go back to the office. The presentations continue all afternoon.

At 5:00pm, Dave says, "OK, thank you everyone. The presentations were really interesting. We will talk about the new products tomorrow. It's a special occasion, so we are all going to go for dinner and drinks at the café bar around the corner. I have to make some phone calls, but I will meet you all there in about half an hour."

8. DINNER AND DRINKS

They all go to the café bar. They find tables and a waitress comes over to them.

"**What can I get you?**" she asks.

"**I'd like** to try some American beer," says Carlos. "**What do you recommend?**"

"**How about** Budweiser?" asks the waitress.

"Yes, OK, a bottle of Budweiser please," says Carlos.

"I'll have the same," says Reggie.

"Your presentation was interesting, Carlos. **I was interested to hear about** your marketing campaign," says Jackie.

"Jackie, stop talking shop!" says Reggie, laughing.

Carlos looks at him. "Sorry? **What does** 'talking shop' **mean?**"

"Talking shop means talking about work. Jackie always talks shop when we go out drinking," says Reggie.

"Oh, I see," says Carlos.

"Sorry," says Jackie. "I love my job, so I always want to talk about it."

"Let's talk about Saturday," says Reggie. "Where do you want to go?"

"Well, I'd like to see the main sights, The Statue of Liberty, Times Square, Central Park, Fifth Avenue…" says Carlos.

"Sure. I can take you to all those places," says Reggie. "Maybe Jihye will like those places too."

"Great. **I'm looking forward to it,**" says Carlos.

They eat and drink a lot. By midnight everyone is very tired. Dave asks the waitress to bring the check.

"How shall we pay?" asks Junya.

"Let's split the check," says Dave.

"What does 'split the check' mean?" asks Ricardo.

"It means we divide the check evenly, so we all pay the same," says Junya.

Everyone gives money to Dave and they all go out into the street. It is midnight, but the streets are very busy. There are many people and cars.

"OK, see you tomorrow at nine, everyone!" says Dave.

"Good night!"

Carlos stops a taxi and gets in. He goes back to his hotel and has a bath.

I had a great day today, but it was very long! he thinks. He soon falls asleep.

9. MORNING MEETING

It is 9:00am. Carlos is sitting in the meeting room with the other managers.

Dave walks in and sits down.

"Good morning, everyone. I hope you had a nice time last night," he says.

"Thank you, yes, we had a really good time," says everyone.

"OK, **let's get started**. So **today, we are going to talk about** new products. **I'm looking forward to hearing your ideas about** new flavours," says Dave. "OK, Carlos, **can you tell us about** your market tests for the apple and grape smoothie and the peach and coconut smoothie?"

"Yes, of course," says Carlos. "We had an idea for a new flavour. It was an apple and grape smoothie. We made some, and tested it in supermarkets with free samples. At first we were happy. People liked the flavour very much. But we had to give up."

"Why?" asks Hans.

"We gave up because one of our competitors started to make an apple and grape smoothie too. They are selling it at a lower price."

"So they undercut us?" asks Jackie.

"**I'm sorry, I didn't catch that. Could you say that again please?**" asks Carlos.

"They undercut us? Do they sell their drinks at a lower price than us?" asks Jackie.

"Yes, that's right. They undercut us. **In my opinion**, our drink tastes better, but when two flavours are the same, customers think about the price," says Carlos." So we tried another flavour. We tried a coconut and peach smoothie."

"How about that?" asks Dave.

"Well, we plan to make it our new product for this year. It will be a very popular drink."

"Why is that?" asks Dave.

"I think it's because it's an unusual flavour, and…"

"**Excuse me for interrupting,** but I think Your Big Drink Company has a similar flavour in Mexico. Don't they sell it in Argentina too?" asks Ricardo.

"No, they don't," says Carlos.

"That's interesting," says Ricardo.

"Yes, we will be the only company selling this flavour in Argentina. I think it will be our best seller," says Carlos.

"So unusual flavours are successful in your market," says Dave.

"Yes, that's right. **I think we should** add more unusual flavours this year and next year," says Carlos.

"I think **I agree with** Carlos," says Jackie. "How does Your Big Drink Company's peach and coconut sell in Mexico, Ricardo?"

"Well, it's popular, but it's not the most popular drink in Mexico. The bestselling drink in Mexico is Dazzle-Oh lime and lemonade. **I agree with** Jackie and Carlos. We should add some more unusual flavours, but I think we should also push our regular flavours. Your Big Drink Company tried to sell more lemonade than us last year. But we sponsored a big soccer match. We gave away T-shirts with Dazzle-oh lime and lemonade on them and…"

"That's very interesting Ricardo," says Dave. "But **for now, let's keep on topic and talk about** ideas for new flavours. Thank you, Carlos. Your story about the market testing of two new flavours was very interesting," says Dave. "**Would you like to add anything else?**"

"**No, I think I've covered everything,**" says Carlos.

"OK, thanks. Next, Jihye, **could you tell us about** plans for new products in Korea?" asks Dave.

"Sure. The Korean market is unique. We have many products with local flavours. Koreans always like something new, so sales are always strong for newer flavours. Please look at the graph on your handout. You can see that sales have been strong for the newer flavours…"

10. DISCUSSING NEW IDEAS

"OK, **let's discuss** ideas for new flavours. **I'd like to hear everyone's opinions,**" says Dave.

"**How about** green tea?" asks Ricardo.

"Well, everyone knows green tea drinks are very popular in Japan, so I think it will be very popular in my market," says Junya. "But I'm not sure about other countries. Maybe they don't drink green tea so much."

"**I disagree,**" says Hans. "Now, green tea is very popular around the world. Many people drink green tea for their health."

"I think so too, but many people also think it is very bitter," says Jihye.

"So how about adding a sweet fruit to it?" asks Carlos. "Green tea and apple, for example."

"**That's a good idea.** Or how about green tea and pear, or peach? We could add some vanilla too," says Hans.

"**What do you think about** this proposal, Jackie?" asks Dave.

"**I think it's a good idea, but we have to think very carefully about** the marketing. We need to give the green tea drink a sweet image."

"**I get your point, but I don't think** we should make it too sweet. Many people drink green tea because they like its bitterness," says Hans.

"It's a good idea," says Dave. "I like it, but I agree with Jackie. **We have to think very carefully about** the image. I'll talk to the factory laboratory now. I'll ask them to make some samples. We can try the samples when we visit the factory this afternoon. So, **let's make a list**. Green tea and apple, green tea and pear, green tea and peach…"

"And maybe we could try adding some vanilla," says Hans.

"Ah yes, vanilla. **Any other ideas?**"

"**How about** green tea and honey?" asks Junya.

"Yes, that also sounds interesting. Let's try that too. OK, **it's nearly** lunchtime. **Let's finish here.** The mini-bus will be outside this building at one pm. Please don't be late."

11. GIVING OPINIONS

Everyone is standing in a laboratory in the factory.

"The laboratory staff worked very hard after I called them," says Dave. "They made samples of all the new flavours we discussed this morning. Let's see how they taste. We'll try this one first. It's green tea and apple," says Dave.

They each take a small cup and drink it.

"**What do you think?**" asks Dave.

"It's not so sweet," says Carlos. "But it has a refreshing taste. I like it. It's nice."

"**I'm afraid I don't agree,**" says Ricardo. "It's a little too bitter for me."

"What do you think, Junya?" asks Dave.

"I like it. We have many green tea products in Japan, but this tastes different."

"**How about this one? What do you think about this?** It's green tea, peach and vanilla," says Dave.

They drink the samples.

"It's nice, but I think the vanilla is a little too strong," says Jihye.

"Do you think so?" asks Carlos. He drinks some more.

"**I get your point.** The vanilla is strong, but I don't think it's too strong. **In my opinion,** it is just right."

"I'm not sure," says Jihye.

"Junya, **How do you feel about it?**" asks Dave.

"I agree with Jihye. The vanilla is a little too strong for me. But it's nice."

"How about we make some more samples with less vanilla?" asks one of the laboratory staff.

"That's a good idea," says Dave. **"While we are waiting, why don't we** try the green tea and pear and the green tea and honey?"

Everyone tries them, but everyone agrees the green tea and apple and the green tea and peach and vanilla taste better.

The laboratory man comes back. "Here you are," he says. "This is green tea, peach and vanilla, but there is not so much vanilla in this sample."

"This is it! This is perfect!" says Junya.

"Yes! I agree!" says Jihye.

"Carlos?" asks Dave.

"I liked the strong vanilla taste, but this is nice too. I can taste the peach more."

"Yes, you're right," says Dave.

"I think this is better," says Hans.

"Does anyone else want to add anything?" asks Dave. "It seems that everyone is happy. OK, we will make some trial samples and do some market research for green tea and apple and green tea, peach and vanilla. **Is that OK with everyone?"** asks Dave.

"Sure. **It's fine with us,"** says everyone.

After the meeting, Carlos talks to Jihye and Reggie.

"So, **what time shall we meet tomorrow?"** asks Carlos.

"How about nine am?" asks Reggie.

"Sure," says Carlos. **"Is that OK with you,** Jihye?"

"Yes, it's fine," says Jihye. **"Where shall we meet?"**

"How about here, outside the office?" asks Reggie.

"OK, **sounds good,"** says Jihye.

"See you tomorrow," says Reggie.

"Yes, **I'm looking forward to it!"** say Carlos and Jihye.

12. SIGHTSEEING

The next morning, Carlos, Jihye and Reggie meet outside the office.

"Good morning! It's a nice day for sightseeing!" says Reggie.

"Yes, it is!" says Carlos. "Where are we going first?"

"Well, I think a sightseeing bus tour is a good idea. We can get a hop on hop off bus."

"Sorry? A what?" asks Jihye.

"A hop on hop off bus. We buy a ticket, and then we can get on the bus and off the bus at different spots around the city. It's very convenient," says Reggie.

"That's a good idea," says Carlos. "Where can we buy tickets?"

"I already bought them. Here you are," says Reggie. He gives Carlos and Jihye the tickets.

"Oh, thank you! **How much do** we **owe you?**" asks Jihye.

"**Don't worry about it.** They weren't so expensive," says Reggie.

"**Are you sure?**" asks Carlos.

"Yes, of course," says Reggie.

"**That's very kind of you.** We will buy you lunch," says Jihye.

"And some beer later!" says Carlos.

Reggie laughs. "Thanks. That will be great!"

They have a very busy day. They get on the bus and visit Times Square. Then, they visit the Empire State Building. They go to the top of the building and enjoy the views.

"Wow! This is amazing!" says Carlos. He takes many photographs. Then, they go to the Statue of Liberty. They take the ferry across to the island. "I've only seen this in movies," says Carlos. "I can't believe I am here!"

He says to another tourist, "**Excuse me, can you take a photo of** me and my colleagues?"

"Sure," says the tourist. Carlos, Reggie and Jihye stand together and the woman takes a photo.

"Are you hungry?" asks Reggie.

"Yes, I am. It's nearly lunchtime," says Carlos.

"Let's stop for lunch," says Reggie.

They go to a Chinese restaurant for lunch. The restaurant is busy, but they get a table near the window. They enjoy watching the people on the street.

"Would you like to do some shopping?" asks Reggie.

"Yes," say Carlos and Jihye.

"Let's go to Macy's department store. It's on the bus route," says Reggie. "Then, we can go to some souvenir shops."

"Excuse me," says Carlos to the waitress. "**Can we have the check please?**"

"Sure," says the waitress. She brings the check.

"**We'll get this**," says Carlos. Jihye and Carlos give the waitress the money.

"Thanks," says Reggie.

"You're welcome," says Carlos.

They spend the afternoon shopping. Carlos buys some souvenirs for the workers in his office. He buys them New York T-shirts, and chocolates. Jihye buys some pens and chocolates for the people in her office.

It is early evening. "Let's go for a few beers," says Carlos.

They go to a bar. When they come out, it is dark.

"We are not so far from Times Square," says Reggie. "Let's go. It's wonderful at night."

They go to Times Square. "Wow!" says Jihye. "This is very different from the morning!" They take some photographs.

"**Thank you so much for today**, Reggie," says Carlos.

"Thank you so much. We **had a wonderful time**," says Jihye.

"You're welcome," says Reggie. "**I'm glad you had a good time. Have a nice flight back home** tomorrow."

"Thank you. **I'll email you when** I get back to the office," says

26

Carlos. "I hope you can come to the Buenos Aires office someday."

"You must come to Seoul too!" says Jihye.

"I hope so!" says Reggie.

They say goodbye. Carlos walks back to his hotel.

13. CHECK-OUT AND DEPARTURE

"Good morning, Sir," says the man on reception.

"Good morning, **I'd like to check out,**" says Carlos.

"OK, **can you tell me your room number please?**"

"Three five six."

"OK, Mr Castro. Thank you. **Here is your receipt. Was everything OK for you?**"

"**Yes, it was fine, thank you,**" says Carlos. "**Can you call me a taxi please?**"

"Sure. A taxi to the airport?"

"Yes please," says Carlos.

The receptionist calls for a taxi. It arrives very quickly.

"**Thank you for staying. We hope to see you again,**" says the receptionist.

"**Thank you,**" says Carlos.

He gets into the taxi and looks out of the window. He thinks about his trip.

I had a very busy few days, he thinks. *It was a great trip, and I made some new friends. I hope I can come back again next year.*

THANK YOU

Thank you for reading A Business Trip to New York. (Word count: 5,679) We hope you enjoyed Carlos's story. Other books in the Useful Phrases series are A Trip to London and A Homestay in Auckland.

There is a quiz about the business phrases in this book on our free study site I Talk You Talk Press EXTRA. http://italk-youtalk.com

If you would like to read more graded readers, please visit our website http://www.italkyoutalk.com

Other Level 1 graded readers include
A Homestay in Auckland
A Trip to London
Dear Ellen
Haruna's Story Part 1
Haruna's Story Part 2
Haruna's Story Part 3
Ken's Story Part 1
Ken's Story Part 2
Life is Surprising!
Strange Stories
The Christmas Present
The Old Hospital
We Met Online

ABOUT THE AUTHOR

I Talk You Talk Press is a Japan-based publisher of language textbooks, graded readers and language learning/teaching resources.

Our team is made up of highly experienced language teachers and translators, who have all studied at least one additional language to an advanced level.

This experience enables us to design our materials from the perspective of both the teacher and the learner. We consult with both teachers and language learners when designing our textbooks and graded readers, and test our materials extensively in the classroom before publication.

We are a fast-growing press, and currently publish graded readers for learners of English. We publish new graded readers monthly.

www.ingramcontent.com/pod-product-compliance
Lightning Source LLC
Chambersburg PA
CBHW032005060426
42449CB00031B/804